NATIONAL GEOGRAPHIC

School Publishing

D0131691

Space

Juan Rueda

PICTURE CREDITS
Illustration by David Legge (14–15).
Cover (all), 11 (above left), 12–13, 16 (above right), NASA;
1, 7 (above left & right), 8, 9 (left), 10 (all), 16 (below left),
Photolibrary.com; 2, 5, 6, 9 (right), 16 (above left, above
center), APL/Corbis; 4, 7 (below left), 11 (right), 16 (below
right), Getty Images.

Produced through the worldwide resources of the National
Geographic Society, John M. Fahey, Jr., President and Chief
Executive Officer; Gilbert M. Grosvenor, Chairman of the
Board; Nina D. Hoffman, Executive Vice President and
President, Books and Education Publishing Group.

PREPARED BY NATIONAL GEOGRAPHIC SCHOOL PUBLISHING
Ericka Markman, Senior Vice President and President Children's
Books and Education Publishing Group; Steve Mico, Senior
Vice President and Publisher; Marianne Hiland, Editorial
Director; Lynnette Brent, Executive Editor; Michael Murphy
and Barbara Wood, Senior Editors; Bea Jackson, Design
Director; David Dumo, Art Director; Margaret Sidlowsky,
Illustrations Director; Matt Wascavage, Manager of
Publishing Services; Sean Philpotts, Production Manager.

MANUFACTURING AND QUALITY MANAGEMENT
Christopher A. Liedel, Chief Financial Officer; Phillip L.
Schlosser, Director; Clifton M. Brown III, Manager.

BOOK DEVELOPMENT
Ibis for Kids Australia Pty Limited.

Published by the National Geographic Society
1145 17th Street, N.W.
Washington, D.C. 20036-4688

ISBN: 0-7922-6068-6

First Printing January 2006
Printed in China

Contents

Think and Discuss   4

Planet Earth   6

The Moon   8

Stars   10

The Sun   11

Our Solar System   12

Use What You Learned   14

Picture Glossary   16

Talk about what you see in the sky. How are day and night different?

moon

stars

Planet Earth

We live on the **planet** called Earth. Earth has light, water, and air.

Earth looks like this from space.

We need light, water, and air to live.

light

water

air

We feel air move when the wind blows.

☾ The Moon

On many nights, we can see the **moon** in the sky.

The moon goes around, or orbits, Earth.

Nothing lives on the moon.
There is no air.
There is no water.

9

Stars

On many nights, we can see **stars** in the sky.

A star is a huge ball of burning gas.

Stars look small from Earth. This is because they are far away.

☀ The Sun

The **sun** is a star.
It is the closest star to Earth.

The sun is very hot.

Warmth and light on Earth come from the sun.

Our Solar System

Earth orbits the sun.
So do other planets.
They are all part of our **solar system**.

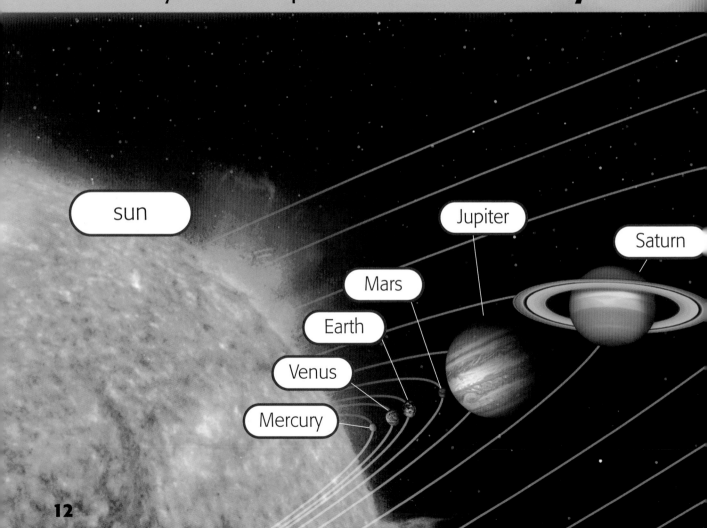

sun

Jupiter

Saturn

Mars

Earth

Venus

Mercury

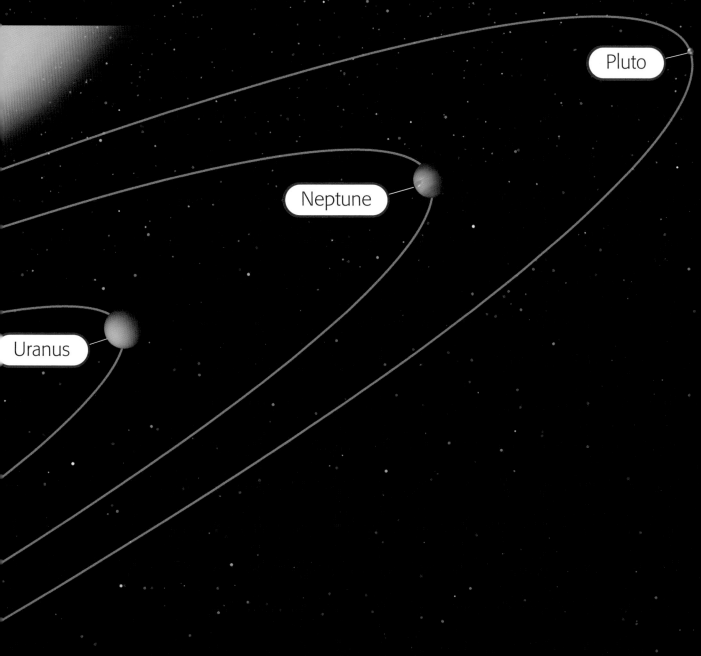

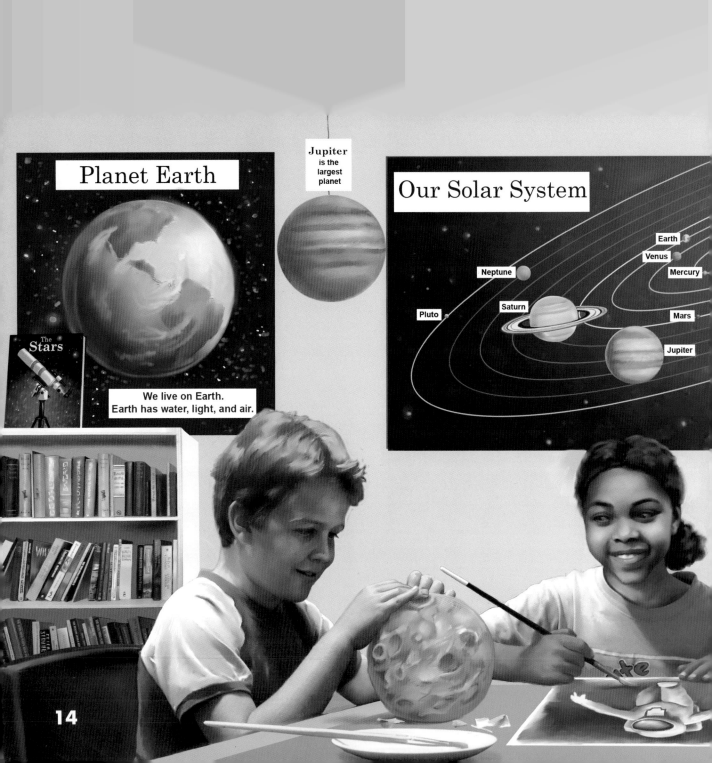

Planet Earth

Jupiter is the largest planet

Our Solar System

We live on Earth.
Earth has water, light, and air.

The Stars

Neptune

Pluto

Saturn

Earth

Venus

Mercury

Mars

Jupiter

Day and Night

day

Earth

moon

night

planet

sky

stars

sun

15

Picture Glossary

Earth

moon

planet

stars

sun